ASHES AND TEARS

WORSHIP RESOURCES FOR ASH WEDNESDAY AND HOLY WEEK

JAMES M. BLOOM

C.S.S. Publishing Co., Inc.

Lima, Ohio

ASHES AND TEARS

Copyright © 1988 by
The C.S.S. Publishing Company, Inc.
Lima, Ohio

Reprinted 1992

You may copy the material in this publication if you are the original purchaser, for use as it was intended (worship material for worship use; educational material for classroom use; dramatic material for staging and production). No additional permission is required from the publisher for such copying by the original purchaser only. Inquiries should be addressed to: The C.S.S. Publishing Company, Inc., 628 South Main Street, Lima, Ohio 45804.

Library of Congress Cataloging-in-Publication Data

Bloom, James M., 1932-
  Ashes and tears.

  1. Ash Wednesday services. 2. Holy Week services. I. Title.
BV485.B56 1988   263'.92   87-27764
ISBN 1-5567-3018-7

8802 / ISBN 0-55673-018-7   PRINTED IN U.S.A.

Table of Contents

Lent	5
Great Day Coming	6
Meditation for Lent *The Way of the Cross*	10
A Different Kind of Communion	16
Ash Wednesday	19
Ash Wednesday Order of Worship	20
A Service of Ashes	22
Palm Sunday	25
Palm Sunday Celebration	26
Maundy Thursday	28
Maundy Thursday Upper Room Communion	29
Maundy Thursday Service (slides, Scripture, and music)	33
Maundy Thursday Meditation *Life's Upper Rooms*	40
Good Friday	43
Service: The Wounds of Christ	44
Community Service for Good Friday	50
A Good Friday Meditation *What About Saturday?*	56

Dedication

These services of worship and meditation are dedicated to Alice Boggs. For most of my ministry she has challenged me and inspired me with her Christian witness. She has been teacher and friend.

Acknowledgments

I am indebted to the congregation of Beechwood United Methodist Church which has given me time to pursue this ministry in the written word. I am also indebted to Rev. Walter Chisholm, pastor of the Norwalk United Methodist Church, for permission to use the Community Good Friday Service included in this publication.

Lent

The period of forty days preceding Easter, not counting Sundays, is called *Lent*. The word originally came from the Anglo-Saxon *lencten*, meaning spring (literally, "to lengthen" [the days]). For the Christian, from the early church until now, it has been a time to reflect on the suffering of Christ and his ultimate victory over the grave. For many, it includes fasting and prayer, two of the great disciplines of the Christian faith.

Lent is a time for Christians to take inventory. It is time to take spiritual assessment of where we are with God. Have we left him out of the picture of our day-to-day living so much that we have forgotten him completely or only call on him in an emergency? Or have we decided that "one of these days" we'll do what he urges us to do, but right now we're doing quite well with our own pursuits? Or, *is God a very present reality* in our every endeavor, undergirding our attempt to move toward spiritual wholeness and health?

If we allow ourselves to do so during this special time of year, we can draw closer to God and he to us. The message of the cross, his suffering and ours, and the inherent new life in the Resurrection will give us new resources to live for him.

Great Day Coming

Forty days of Lent sounds like a long time when you begin it. Soon, it passes. Lent is gone and Holy Week is upon us and we look forward to Resurrection Sunday, Easter. There are many precedents for the forty days in Scripture: Noah upon the flood, Jesus in the wilderness of temptation, Moses on the mount for forty days, Israel in the wilderness for forty years. It climaxes with *Holy Week*.

Palm Sunday began what is called Holy Week. With all the joy and spectacle of a parade, Jesus and his followers made their way to the temple in Jerusalem as if he really were a conquering king. After all, he had conquered their hearts and allegiance. When the hoopla was over, they went to Bethany to rest for the night. So the first day ended. Great day coming!

Monday Early Monday morning they made their way along the same route out of Bethany (meaning *house of dates*) and passed through Bethphage (meaning *house of figs*), back to the temple.

Jesus stopped by a fig tree. He cursed it for being unproductive, even though it was not the season for figs. It is difficult to understand why Jesus did this. Some say that you can tell, even out of season, if a fig tree will bear, because of a precursor bud. Jesus apparently knew that this fig tree was barren. The only way we can legitimize his action is in recognizing that it was an enacted parable: Jesus wants us to bear fruit always, in season and out.

He went into the temple. There, in another burst of anger, he *overturned the tables of the money-changers and the seats of those who sold pigeons. He said to them, "It is written, 'My house shall be called a house of prayer'; but you make it a den of robbers."* It took place in the Court of the Gentiles. People from afar had foreign money to exchange and were being charged excessively. Even pigeons, the smallest allowable sacrifice, was out of range for the poor. So ended the second day, and Jesus and the Twelve most likely returned to Bethany. Great day coming!

Tuesday On Tuesday Jesus taught in the temple courts. It was as though he were unafraid after the previous day's events. He openly answered those who raised questions with him: "By what authority are you doing these things?" "Is it lawful to pay taxes to Caesar, or not?" A widow marries her husband's brother; he dies. She marries each of seven brothers; they all die. Then she dies. Whose wife will she be in the resurrection? Which is the great commandment in the law?"

He countered with a question, "The baptism of John, did it come from heaven, or men?" They could not answer for fear of incriminating themselves, or for fear of the people who revered John. So he told them nothing about his authority.

Taking a coin, he said, "Render therefore to Caesar the things that are Caesar's and to God the things that are God's." "In the resurrection they neither marry nor are given in marriage . . ." "You shall love the Lord your God with all your heart, and with all your soul, and with all your mind . . . you shall love your neighbor as yourself."

The decision was made on Tuesday to get rid of Jesus. Later, in the Garden of Gethsemane, he said to his captors, "Have you come out as against a robber, with swords and clubs to capture me? Day after day I sat in the temple teaching, and you did not seize me. But all this has taken place, that the scriptures of the prophets might be fulfilled." (Matthew 26:55-56)

He and the disciples went to the Mount of Olives. The third day ended. Great day coming!

Wednesday Wednesday was spent in Bethany. Simon the Leper invited Jesus to come and have a meal with him. Perhaps out of gratitude for Jesus' healing, he played host. (He is spoken of as Simon the leper in Matthew 26:6 and as Simon the Pharisee in Luke 7:36-50.) While there, a woman of ill repute came, anointing Jesus with expensive perfume. Above much objection, Jesus honored her act as one of anointing for his burial. Judas, one of the objectors, went later that day to the chief priests to betray Jesus. So ended Wednesday, the fourth day. Great day coming!

Thursday It was the day of preparation for the Passover. It was the first day of the Feast of Unleavened Bread. (Mark 14:17-26) It was the Last Meal before Jesus' death that he had with his disciples. After the supper, Jesus took his disciples, who had just asked, one after another, "Is it I?" to pray in the Garden of Gethsemane, at the foot of the Mount of Olives. He went to pray in the garden "as was his custom," seeking strength in prayer and yielding himself to the will of God.

It was in the garden that the betrayer Judas came, using a time-honored custom to greet a friend, to betray him. For thirty pieces of silver, the price of a slave, Jesus was betrayed, arrested, and taken to the High Priest for trial. The fifth day ended. Great day coming!

Friday This was the day of Christ's crucifixion, the Friday we call good. In the early morning hours, under the cover of darkness, the foul deed was accomplished. He had several trials before judgment was made. He was passed like a hot potato from the High Priest, Caiaphas, to Pontius Pilate to Herod, back to Pontius Pilate. The charge was changed from blasphemy against God to treason against the state. It was this last charge that sent him to the cross. As one last ironic act, Pilate placed above his cross, in Latin, Hebrew, and Greek, "Jesus of Nazareth, King of the Jews." The disciples scattered — except for John. In death, Joseph of Arimathea, a secret disciple and a Pharisee who would not vote for Jesus' death, took his body and placed it in his own tomb. It was the body of one sacrificed at the very moment the innocent lambs were slaughtered for temple sacrifice (according to John's Gospel).

So ended another day, the sixth day of Holy Week. Great day coming!

Saturday And what about Saturday? Not much was said. The disciples hid, fearing for their own safety. Mary the mother of Jesus, Mary Magdalene, and Salome bought spices after Sabbath to anoint Jesus' body. Confusion and fear and grief were the order of the day. Their hopes for a new day and a new world had been dashed. There was no evidence that anyone really believed that he would rise from the grave. Soldiers guarded that tomb for fear that someone would steal his body and spread the lie that he had risen. It was Holy Saturday. Great day coming!

Sunday But when Sunday came, it was a different story. Confusion and fear turned to joy and hope and belief. First he appeared alive to Mary Magdalene, to Mary the mother of James, Salome, John and Peter, the two men on the road to Emmaus, and to the eleven. Even to as many as five hundred he appeared. There were other appearances as well. Might we, like Paul, say that he appeared also to each of us as one untimely born? When Sunday comes, all the rest of the week makes sense. God highly exalts those who come in faith and obedience.

> *Have this mind among yourselves,*
> *which is yours in Christ Jesus,*
> *who, though he was in the form of God,*
> *did not count equality with God a thing to be grasped,*
> *but emptied himself, taking the form of a servant,*
> *being born in the likeness of men.*
> *And being found in human form*
> *he humbled himself and became obedient unto death,*
> *even death on a cross.*
> *Therefore God has highly exalted him and bestowed on him*
> *the name which is above every name,*
> *that at the name of Jesus every knee should bow,*
> *in heaven and on earth and under the earth,*
> *and every tongue confess that Jesus Christ is Lord,*
> *to the glory of God the Father.*   *(Philippians 2:5-11)*

It's Sunday — Resurrection Day. When you really think about it, it's bigger and better than we ever dreamed. It changed history. He can change us. *Great day coming! Alleluia!*

Meditation for Lent

The Way of the Cross

Mark 8:31-38

Introduction

Mark 8:31-38 comes immediately after the great confession of Peter that Jesus is the Christ, the anointed One of God, the very Son of God. In another Gospel Jesus proclaims that this insight did not come to Peter by flesh and blood alone. No human being had told him. The human beings in that day had several ideas about the Messiah. Most of them were not consistent with Jesus' view of himself nor with the way he was to conduct himself in the role of Messiah. I am indebted to the scholarship of William Barclay for some basic ideas of what people were thinking when they considered the Christ.

Most of them dreamed of another David who would come as a conquering king and drive out the enemy, now Rome. When the last king was carried away to Assyria and later Babylon, the independent nation of the twelve tribes was at an end. Ten tribes totally disappeared. Those captive in Babylon were able to return to Jerusalem under the reign and goodwill of Cyrus the Persian, but still as a conquered nation. Next came the Greeks and the Romans.

In their dreams and apocalyptic literature, written between the Old and New Testaments, were steps to the coming of the Messianic Age. First, they believed that before the Messiah came there would be a time of terrible travail. (2 Esdras 9:3) — "Quakings of places, tumult of peoples, schemings of nations, confusion of leaders, disquietude of princes." The Jewish Mishna states that when the Messiah is near, "arrogance increases, ambition shoots up, that the vine yields fruit yet wine is dear. The government turns to heresy. There is no instruction. The synagogue is devoted to lewdness. Galilee is destroyed; Gabian laid waste. The inhabitants of a district go from city to city without finding compassion. The wisdom of the learned is hated, the godly despised, truth is absent. Boys insult old men, old men stand in the presence of children. The son depreciates the father, the daughter rebels against the mother, the daughter-in-law against the mother-in-law. A man's enemies are his housefellows."

Into this chaos would come Elijah as forerunner and herald of the Christ. Then the Messiah would come. The word *Messiah* is Hebrew for the Anointed One. The word *Christ* is Greek for the same word. A king was made king by anointing. The Messiah was God's Anointed King. When the Messiah came, the nations would ally themselves together in battle against the champion of God. (4 Ezra 13:33-35) "It shall be when all the nations hear his (The Messiah's) voice, every man shall leave his own land and the warfare they have against one another, and an innumerable multitude shall be gathered together desiring to fight against him." The result will be that the Messiah will utterly destroy these hostile powers. Again 4 Ezra says in 12:32, 33, "He shall reprove them for their ungodliness, rebuke them for the unrighteousness, reproach them to their faces with their treacheries. And when he has rebuked them he shall destroy them.

Following this event, when all the enemies of the Messiah and Israel have been destroyed, there will be a renovation of Jerusalem. It will be the new Jerusalem come down from heaven. The Jews dispersed will gather in the new Jerusalem. The eleventh Psalm of Solomon pictures that return gloriously.

Blow ye in Zion on the trumpet to summon the saints,
Cause ye to be heard in Jerusalem the voice of him that
bringeth good tidings; For God hath pity on Israel
in visiting them.
Stand on the height, O Jerusalem, and behold thy children.

> *From the East and the West, gathered together by the Lord;*
> *From the North they come in the gladness of their God,*
> *From the isles afar off God hath gathered them.*
> *High mountains hath he abased into a plain for them;*
> *The hills fled at their entrance.*
> *The woods gave them shelter as they passed by;*
> *Every sweet-smelling tree God caused to spring up for them,*
> *That Israel might pass by in the visitation of the glory of their god.*
> *Put on, O Jerusalem, thy glorious garments;*
> *Make ready thy holy robe;*
> *For God hath spoken good for Israel forever and ever,*
> *Let the Lord do what he hath spoken concerning Israel and Jerusalem;*
> *Let the Lord raise up Israel by His glorious name.*
> *The mercy of the Lord be upon Israel forever and ever.*

Palestine would be the world center and all the world subject to it. Under its rule, through the Messiah, would come a new age of peace and goodness. This was the kind of thinking that the disciples were used to all their lives. They thought of him in terms of irresistible conquest. Judas Iscariot really believed it, as did others. You can see it even in Peter, as Jesus hits them with a staggering idea.

1. Jesus Says No to the Common Thoughts About the Messiah

He picks up a theme that had been long forgotten, that of a suffering servant of God. Jesus came that he might fulfill the words of Isaiah.

> *The Spirit of the Lord is upon me, because he has anointed me to preach good news to the poor. He has sent me to proclaim release to the captives and recovering of sight to the blind, to set at liberty those who are oppressed, to proclaim the acceptable year of the Lord. (Luke 4:18, 19)*

All his life and ministry he had been engaged in the business of healing the broken bodies and the broken souls of men, women, and children. Perhaps he even saw himself in the role of the lamb, slain for the atonement of not only the Jews but for all people. Later, the author of the book of Hebrews pictured him as both High Priest who offered the sacrifice and the Lamb that was sacrificed. He says in the tenth chapter, vv. 11-14:

> *And every priest stands daily at his service, offering repeatedly the same sacrifices, which can never take away sins. But when Christ had offered for all time a single sacrifice for sins, he sat down at the right hand of God, then to wait until his enemies should be made a stool for his feet. For by a single offering he has perfected for all time those who are sanctified.*

The disciples were appalled that Jesus would even talk about a sacrifice of his life. They were also afraid for their own lives. They knew the threats of death upon Jesus' life by those in power. Peter was bold to speak. Matthew quotes Peter as saying, "God forbid, Lord! This shall never happen to you." (16:22) Satan returned to tempt Jesus in the form of a close friend. Jesus consistently avoided the easy way. He knew that in order to fulfill his calling he had to walk the way of sacrifice, the way of the cross.

He did not yield to the temptation to be at ease with his popularity in Galilee. He reproached the very center of power that controlled the lives of people, that did not allow them to grow into God, that kept them enslaved to their sins. He rebuked Peter and all of us who take the easy way out. His way is the way of the cross and he bids us to take up that way, too. "He called the crowd to Him, together with His disciples, and said to them, 'If anyone wishes to come after me, let him deny himself, and let him take up his cross, and let him follow me.' " (Mark 8:34, 35, Barclay) Dietrich Bonhoeffer, the great German Christian who fought Hitler and died at the hands of the Nazis just days before the war was over, called what God is about in Jesus Christ a "costly grace." It cost Jesus his life. He said in his *The Cost of Discipleship*, that many of us are content with "cheap grace." He further stated, *Cheap grace is the preaching of forgiveness without requiring repentance, baptism without church discipline, Communion without confession, absolution without contrition. Cheap grace is grace without discipleship, grace without a cross, grace without Jesus Christ, living and incarnate.*

Costly grace is the treasure hidden in the field; for the sake of it a man will gladly go and sell all he has. It is the pearl of great price to buy which the merchant will sell all his goods. It is the kingly rule of Christ, for whose sake a man will pluck out his eye which causes him to stumble, it is the call of Jesus Christ at which the disciple leaves his nets and follows him. . . . Above all, it is costly because it cost God the life of his Son: "ye were bought at a price," and what has cost God much cannot be cheap for us. (*The Cost of Discipleship*, **pp. 38, 39.**)

2. The Test of Our Discipleship

In the very center of our heart, mind, will, and strength is how far we are willing to go the way of the cross with Jesus. It first involves our being willing to shed tears over our sins. He calls us to repent, all of us, because we have all sinned and come short of God's will for our lives. Then we are to be servants. We are to be self-giving, not keeping all things for ourselves. What about the dangerous assignments God might give us? Are we willing to lay down our lives for the cause of Christ? Most of us will never have to die physically for Christ's sake. Yet if we truly die to self, we will also be open to anything God wishes of us.

There is a story from the fourth century A.D. about a monk named Telemachus. He determined that the best way to serve God was to leave the world he knew and live alone in fasting, prayer, and meditation. He thought that would save his soul. But in his contemplation he felt something was wrong. One day he rose from prayer to realize he had been selfish; he had become aware that to serve God was to serve humankind. He left the desert and went to the city of Rome. Rome was now a Christian city, but some of the old sins remained. The gladiatorial games continued to make a Roman holiday for the people. Christians were no longer thrown to the lions, but those captured in war had to fight and kill each other. Telemachus was appalled when he saw what was going on. He jumped into the arena and became a barrier between the combatants. Men for whom Christ died were killing each other to amuse an allegedly Christian populace. The crowds began to throw stones at Telemachus, still in his hermit's robes. They urged the gladiators to kill him and get him out of the way. A gladiator's sword rose, flashed, and stabbed. Telemachus lay dead. Suddenly the crowd was silent. They realized what they had done. The games ended abruptly that day, and never began again. Telemachus, by his death, had ended them. He had served his God by laying down his life for his fellows.

"What profit is it for a man to gain the whole world and to forfeit his life? For what is a man to give in exchange for his life?" (Mark 8:37, Barclay) Our life is not determined by what we have, but in terms of who we are when it comes to following Christ. Do we have the strength and the will to do those impossible things which will bring Jesus Christ and his peace to the hearts of mankind? We may have to be like Telemachus, like the Christ before him, who stands in the breach between those who would fight to the death, and end up being killed ourselves. Jesus Christ stood in the breach between evil men in order to bring salvation to us. It meant the way of the cross for him; it will mean no less for us.

A Different Kind of Communion

(*Congregation stand)

PRELUDE

***CALL TO WORSHIP**
    Pastor: Everyone who thirsts,
    People: Come to the water;
    Pastor: And he who has no money,
    People: Come, buy, and eat.

***INVOCATION**

***HYMN**   "Come, Thou Fount of Every Blessing"

OLD TESTAMENT READING   Isaiah 44:1-5

SILENT REFLECTION

EPISTLE READING   Philippians 2:1-11

SILENT REFLECTION

PSALM PRAYER
    Pastor: To thee, O Lord, I lift up my soul.
    People: O my God, in thee I trust,
    Pastor: Make me to know thy ways, O Lord; teach me thy paths.
    People: Lead me in thy truth, and teach me, for thou art the God of my salvation; for thee I wait all the day long.
    Pastor: Be mindful of thy mercy, O Lord, and of thy steadfast love, for they have been from of old.
    People: Remember not the sins of my youth, or my transgressions; according to thy steadfast love remember me, for thy goodness' sake, O Lord!

Pastor: Oh guard my life, and deliver me; let me not be put to shame, for I take refuge in thee.

People: **May integrity and uprightness preserve me, for I wait for thee.**

(Psalm 25:1-2, 4-7, 20-21)

OFFERTORY

*DOXOLOGY AND PRAYER OF DEDICATION

ANTHEM

SILENT PRAYER

*HYMN   *"I Would Be True"* [or another appropriate hymn]
(Remain standing for reading of Gospel)

*GOSPEL   John 4:7-15

SILENT REFLECTION

SERMON   *The Water That Satisfies*

INVITATION TO CLEANSING

Seek the Lord while he may be found,
call upon him while he is near;
let the wicked forsake his way,
and the unrighteous man his thoughts;
let him return to the Lord,
that he may have mercy on him,
and to our God, for he will abundantly pardon.

(Isaiah 55:6-7)

This day we invite you to come forward one by one to receive a cup of cold water. As you drink it, may it not only quench your thirst, but also refresh your Spirit.

(Soft, prayerful music as people come forward; as each drinks from their cup, the pastor may say, "A cup of water in Jesus' name."
When all have communed and returned to their seats, continue the service.)

PRAYER OF DEDICATION

*HYMN　　　　　　　　*"All the Way My Savior Leads Me"*
　　　　　　　　　　　　　　　　[or another appropriate hymn]

*BENEDICTION Go forth in joy,
　　　　　and be led forth in peace.

POSTLUDE

[Instructions: This can be done very simply by providing a punch bowl full of cool water on a stand. Use a ladle to dip water into small paper cups.]

Ash Wednesday

Ash Wednesday begins Lent in the Western church. It represents the penitence by which we come to God. From the Middle Ages it has been characterized by the imposition of ashes on the forehead of individuals; some impose the sign of the cross. Some take the ashes from the burning of the previous year's palm leaves. Ashes were applied to the body at times of fasting as a sign of penitence; this was an Old Testament rite of purification. It was often associated with sackcloth and dust at the time of mourning.

The writer of Hebrews says:

For if the sprinkling of defiled persons with the blood of goats and bulls and with the ashes of a heifer sanctifies for the purification of the flesh, how much more shall the blood of Christ, who through the eternal Spirit offered himself without blemish to God, purify your conscience from dead works to serve the living God.

(9:13, 14)

For most of us, ashes remain a symbol of our confession of sin and our sorrow for it.

Jesus challenges the people — and us — in the Sermon on the Mount:

"And when you fast, do not look dismal, like the hypocrites, for they disfigure their faces that their fasting may be seen by men. [They put on sackcloth and ashes.] Truly, I say to you, they have received their reward. But when you fast, anoint your head and wash your face, that your fasting may not be seen by men but by your Father who is in secret; and your Father who sees in secret will reward you."

(Matthew 6:16-18)

Ash Wednesday Order of Worship

(*Congregation stand)

GATHERING

PRELUDE

GREETING

Pastor:	The grace of our Lord Jesus Christ be with you.
People:	**And also with you.**
Pastor:	Bless the Lord, O my soul, and all that is within me bless God's holy name.
People:	**Bless the Lord, O my soul, and forget not all God's benefits.**
Pastor:	Who forgives all your sins and heals all your infirmities;
People:	**Who redeems your life from the grave, and crowns you with mercy and loving kindness.**

OPENING PRAYER (in unison)

Most holy God, your Son came to save sinners;
We come to this season of repentence,
   confessing our unworthiness,
   asking for new and honest hearts,
   and the healing power of your forgiveness.
Grant this through Christ our Lord. Amen

*HYMN   *"Come, Every Soul by Sin Oppressed"*
                                        [or another suitable hymn]

ACT OF PRAISE

Pastor:	Out of the depths I cry to thee, O Lord!
People:	**Lord, hear my voice! Let thy ears be attentive to the voice of my supplications!**
Pastor:	If thou, O Lord, shouldst mark iniquities, Lord, who could stand?

People:	**But there is forgiveness with thee, that thou mayest be feared.**
Pastor:	I wait for the Lord, my soul waits, and in his word I hope;
People:	**My soul waits for the Lord more than watchmen for the morning.**
Pastor:	Israel, hope in the Lord! For with the Lord there is steadfast love, and with him is plenteous redemption.
People:	**And he will redeem Israel from all his iniquities.**

OFFERING, DOXOLOGY, AND PRAYER

ANTHEM

GOSPEL Matthew 6:1-6, 16-21

MESSAGE *Sackcloth and Ashes*

INVITATION TO THE OBSERVANCE OF LENTEN DISCIPLINE

THANKSGIVING OVER THE ASHES

IMPOSITION OF ASHES (Those who wish may come forward to have the sign of the cross imposed on their foreheads.)

*HYMN *"Breathe on Me, Breath of God"*

*BENEDICTION
Send us forth, O God, in humble dependence on you, that we may walk in strength, faith, love, and hope, in simple obedience to your will. Amen

POSTLUDE

A Service of Ashes

(*Congregation stand)

PRELUDE

*CALL TO WORSHIP
"And when you fast, do not look dismal, like the hypocrites, for they disfigure their faces that their fasting may be seen by men. Truly, I say to you, they have their reward. But when you fast, anoint your head and wash your face, that your fasting may not be seen by men but by your Father who is in secret; and your Father who sees in secret will reward you."
(Matthew 6:16-18)

*UNISON PRAYER
Almighty and everlasting God, who hatest nothing that thou hast made, and dost forgive the sins of all those who are penitent; Create and make in us new and contrite hearts, that we, worthily lamenting our sins and acknowledging our wretchedness, may obtain of thee, the God of all mercy, perfect remission and forgiveness; through Jesus Christ our Lord. Amen
(Ash Wednesday Collect from *The Book of Common Prayer*, 1952.)

HYMN   *"Joyful, Joyful, We Adore Thee"*
[or another suitable hymn]

THE CALL TO REPENTANCE

Pastor: "Yet even now," says the Lord, "return to me with all your heart, with fasting, with weeping, and with mourning; and rend our hearts and not your garments."

People: Return to the Lord, your God, for he is gracious and merciful, slow to anger, and abounding in steadfast love, and repents of evil.

Pastor and People: *Blow the trumpet in Zion; sanctify a fast; call a solemn assembly; gather the people.*

SILENT PRAYER

CHRIST'S HIGH-PRIESTLY PRAYER   John 17:1b-16
"Father, the hour is come."

*HYMN   *"Dear Lord and Father of Mankind"*

OFFERTORY

*DOXOLOGY AND PRAYER OF DEDICATION

ANTHEM

SERMON   *A Broken and Contrite Heart*
(based on Psalm 51:6-17)

INVITATION TO HEALING
  Tonight we will not, like Zion's citizens of old, put on sackcloth and ashes. It was a symbol of repentance. Let us come with broken and contrite hearts. As you come forward, there are two bowls, one empty and one filled with water. In the empty bowl literally throw away some sin, some hurt, some distress, some confusion. Then place your hands in the water; let the Spirit of Christ cleanse you. As pastor, instead of placing an ashen cross on your forehead, I will form a cross on your forehead with anointing oil for the healing of your soul.
  (Silence as people come forward when they feel led by the Holy Spirit. May the silence be a time of prayer.)

*CLOSING PRAYER   (Form circle, linked hand-in-hand, around perimeter of sanctuary)

*HYMN   *"They'll Know We Are Christians by Our Love"*
[or another suitable hymn]

*BENEDICTION
   The Lord bless you and keep you,
   The Lord make his face to shine upon you,
      and be gracious to you.
   The Lord lift up his countenance upon you,
      and give you peace.

POSTLUDE

Palm Sunday

The first day of Holy Week commemorates Jesus' triumphal entry into the city of Jerusalem. He was met with a crowd waving palm branches and laying their garments to make a pathway for their King.

> *Rejoice greatly, O daughter of Zion!*
> *Shout aloud, O daughter of Jerusalem!*
> *Lo, your king comes to you;*
> *triumphant and victorious is he,*
> *humble and riding on an ass,*
> *on a colt the foal of an ass.* (9:9)

to which they responded:

> "Hosanna! Blessed is he who comes in the name of the Lord! Blessed is the Kingdom of our father David that is coming! Hosanna in the highest!"
> (Mark 11:9b-10)

Palm Sunday Celebration

(*Congregation stand)

PRELUDE

CHORAL CALL TO WORSHIP
"O Worship the King"

PERIOD OF SILENT PRAYER
"Be still and know that I am God." (Psalm 46:10)

*PROCESSIONAL HYMN
"All Glory, Laud, and Honor"
(Adult and children's choirs waving palms as they process; receptacles at front in which to place palms.)

*CALL TO WORSHIP (in unison)
Let us wave the palms;
Let us sing the songs;
Let us prepare a pathway for our King.
Hallelujah!
Let us praise Jesus our Christ and King.

*COLLECT
Almighty God, we give thanks for the Master who rode in triumph into the city of his fathers. We praise you that he came as the conqueror, not of force and military might but of love and peace. In the spirit of those who sang "Hosanna to the Son of David" so long ago, we join that great chorus of those who confess Jesus Christ as Lord, to the glory of your name. Amen

APOSTLES' CREED

PASTORAL PRAYER

OFFERTORY

*DOXOLOGY AND PRAYER OF DEDICATION

CHILDREN'S CHOIR
    "Hosanna, Loud Hosanna"   [or other suitable music]

CHILDREN'S STORY

*HYMN   *"Guide Me, O Thou Great Jehovah"*

SCRIPTURE READING   **John 12:12-19**

ANTHEM   *"The Palms"*

SERMON
    Behold, Your King Is Coming   (John 12:15)

CALL TO FOLLOW JESUS CHRIST

*RECESSIONAL HYMN
    "Come, Ye That Love the Lord"
    (Adult and children's choirs take palms from receptacles and wave as they leave.)

*BENEDICTION

POSTLUDE

Maundy Thursday

The Thursday of Holy Week is one of the earliest celebration of the Christian church. The word "Maundy" comes from the Latin *mandatum* meaning "commandment." It comes from the statement of Jesus in the Upper Room, "A new commandment I give to you, that you love one another; even as I have loved you, that you also love one another. By this all men will know that you are my disciples, if you have love for one another." (John 13:34-35)

As we celebrate Maundy Thursday, we observe the Last Supper of our Lord. In Jesus' observing the Passover feast with his disciples, the Sacrament of Holy Communion is given birth. For the most part, it is a solemn service which prepares us for the crucifixion of our Lord.

Maundy Thursday
Upper Room Communion

PRELUDE

PROCEDURE ANNOUNCEMENT: Tonight we will be observing Holy Communion in a manner reminding us of the night when Jesus gathered with the twelve disciples in an upper room. When the time in the service indicates, the ushers will guide us, in groups of twelve, to a room set apart that we may commune with our Lord.

CALL TO WORSHIP

Pastor: "Hear, O Israel: The Lord our God is one Lord; and you shall love the Lord your God with all your soul, and with all your might."

People: His words shall be in our hearts, and we will teach our children diligently. We shall talk of them in our house. They shall be a pattern for our living.

Pastor: It is the Lord our God who brought us out of the land of Egypt, out of the house of bondage.

People: Deliver us, O Lord God, from the slavery of sin.

*****HYMN**   *"Guide Me, O Thou Great Jehovah"*

Lay Reader: Why is this night different from all other nights? On all other nights we eat either leavened or unleavened bread. Why on this night do we eat only unleavened bread? On all other nights we eat all kinds of herbs. Why on this night do we eat especially bitter herbs? On all other nights we do not dip herbs in any condiment. Why on this night do we dip them in salt water and haroses? On all other nights we eat without special festivities. Why on this night do we hold this Passover service?

Pastor: The Syrian pursued our fathers who went down into Egypt and sojourned there in a very small number, and grew into a nation great and of an infinite multitude. The Egyptians afflicted us and persecuted us, laying on us most grievous burdens. And we cried to the Lord God of our fathers, who heard us, and looked down on our afflictions, labor, and distress. And he brought us out of Egypt with a strong hand, and an outstretched arm, with great terror, with signs and wonders. Therefore, even if all of us were wise and well versed in the Torah, it would be our duty from year to year to tell the story of our deliverance from Egypt. Indeed, to dwell at length on it is accounted praiseworthy.

PRAYER OF CONFESSION

PSALM PRAYER

Pastor: O give thanks to the Lord, call on his name, make known his deeds among the peoples!

People: **He is the Lord our God; his judgments are in all the earth.**

Pastor: He is mindful of his covenant for ever, of the word that he commanded, for a thousand generations.

People: **Israel came to Egypt; Jacob sojourned in the land of Ham. And the Lord made his**

	people very fruitful, and made them stronger than their foes. He turned their hearts to hate his people, to deal graftily with his servants.
Pastor:	He sent Moses his servant, and Aaron whom he had chosen. They wrought his signs among them, and miracles in the land of Ham.
People:	**He sent darkness, and made the land dark; they rebelled against his words.**
Pastor:	He turned their waters into blood, and caused their fish to die. Their land swarmed with frogs, even in the chambers of their kings.
People:	**He smote their vines and fig trees, and shattered the trees of their country.**
Pastor:	He smote all the first-born in their land, the first issue of all their strength.
People:	**Then he led forth Israel with silver and gold, and there was none among the tribes who stumbled.**
Pastor:	Egypt was glad when they departed, for dread of them had fallen upon it.
People:	**He spread a cloud for a covering, and fire to give light by night.**
Pastor:	They asked, and he brought quails, and gave them bread from heaven in abundance.
People:	**He opened the rock, and water gushed forth; it flowed through the desert like a river.**
Pastor:	For he remembered his holy promise, and Abraham his servant.
People:	**So he led forth his people with joy, his chosen ones with singing.**

Pastor:	And he gave them the lands of the nations; and they took possession of the fruit of the peoples' toil.
People:	**To the end that they should keep his statutes, and observe his laws.**
All:	*Praise the Lord!*

(Psalm 105:1, 7-8, 23-29, 33, 36-45)

ANTHEM

INVITATION TO COMMUNE

SCRIPTURE   Mark 14:12-17

UPPER ROOM COMMUNION
(Follow the direction of ushers. You will be led to an "Upper Room" where you will observe the Last Supper with our Lord. Go as silently as you can.)

[Pastor may dress in costume as Jesus and administer the sacrament with the words of Jesus in the Upper Room.]

READING OF LAST SUPPER SCRIPTURES
(Selections from John 14, 15, 16, 17 may be read by selected readers while small groups move in and out of the "Upper Room." Special music may also be provided until all have communed.)

*HYMN   *"Love Divine, All Loves Excelling"*

*BENEDICTION
This is my commandment, that you love one another as I have loved you. Greater love has no man than this, that a man lay down his life for his friends. You are my friends if you do what I command you.

(John 15:12-14)

POSTLUDE

Maundy Thursday Service

(*Congregation stands)

Preparation: This service combines the use of color slides with Scripture and music. You may wish to substitute slides that are more appropriate for you. When it comes to Communion in the Upper Room, you may wish to direct the congregation to a room adjacent to the sanctuary, by groups of twelve. There can be special music at this time or soft organ music.

[Before service . . . Picture of head of Christ projected on screen]

PRELUDE

CALL TO WORSHIP

*HYMN   *"When I Survey the Wondrous Cross"*

READING OF SCRIPTURE   Luke 22:7-13

Then came the day of Unleavened Bread, on which the passover lamb had to be sacrificed. So Jesus sent Peter and John, saying, "Go and prepare the passover for us, that we may eat it." They said to him, "Where will you have us prepare it?" He said to them, "Behold, when you have entered the city, a man carrying a jar of water will meet you; follow him into the house which he enters, and tell the householder, 'The Teacher says to you, Where is the guest room, where I am to eat the passover with my disciples?' And he will show you a large upper room furnished; there make ready." And they went, and found it as he had told them; and they prepared the passover.

EVENING PRAYER

ANTHEM

READING OF SCRIPTURE   **Luke 22:14-20**

And when the hour came, he sat at table, and the apostles with him.

[Project slide of Last Supper]

And he said to them, "I have earnestly desired to eat this passover with you before I suffer; for I tell you I shall not eat it until it is fulfilled in the kingdom of God." And he took a cup, and when he had given thanks he said, "Take this, and divide it among yourselves; for I tell you that from now on I shall not drink of the fruit of the vine until the kingdom of God comes." And he took bread, and when he had given thanks he broke it and gave it to them, saying, "This is my body."

INVITATION TO COMMUNE

For you who are weary and heavy-laden; for you who have sinned and bear the weight of its guilt; for you who seek God's love in a new and special way; for you who would turn away from the power of this world and want the power of his Spirit in your life, come now to the table of our Lord.

COMMUNION IN THE UPPER ROOM

[Groups of twelve at the guidance of ushers; special music or soft organ music; possible selected readings; then, after all have communed]

READING OF SCRIPTURE   **Mark 14:32-42**

And they went to a place which was called Gethsemane; and he said to his disciples, "Sit here, while I pray."

[Slide of Jesus praying in Gethsemane]

And he took with him Peter and James and John, and began to be greatly distressed and troubled. And he said to them, "My soul is very sorrowful, even to

death; remain here, and watch." And going a little farther, he fell on the ground and prayed that, if it were possible, the hour might pass from him. And he said, "Abba, Father, all things are possible to thee; remove this cup from me; yet not what I will, but what thou wilt." And he came and found them sleeping, for their eyes were very heavy; and they did not know what to answer him. And he came a third time, and said to them, "Are you still sleeping and taking your rest? It is enough; the hour has come; the Son of man is betrayed into the hands of sinners. Rise, let us be going; see, my betrayer is at hand."

HYMN " 'Tis Midnight and on Olive's Brow"
[or another suitable hymn]

READING OF SCRIPTURE
    Reader #1   (Luke 22:47-53)
   While he was still speaking, there came a crowd, and the man called Judas, one of the twelve, was leading them.
   [Slide of Judas kissing Jesus]
   He drew near to Jesus to kiss him; but Jesus said to him, "Judas, would you betray the Son of man with a kiss?" And when those who were about him saw what would follow, they said, "Lord, shall we strike with the sword?" And one of them struck the slave of the high priest and cut off his right ear. But Jesus said, "No more of this!" And he touched his ear and healed him. Then Jesus said to the chief priests . . . and elders, who had come out against him, "Have you come out as against a robber, with swords and clubs? When I was with you day after day in the

temple, you did not lay hands on me. But this is your hour, and the power of darkness."

Reader #2 (Luke 22:54)
Then they seized him and led him away, bringing him into the high priest's house.

Reader #1 (Luke 22:55-62)
Peter followed at a distance; and when they kindled a fire in the . . . courtyard and sat down together, Peter sat among them.

[Slide of Peter warming himself by the fire]

Then a maid, seeing him as he sat in the light and gazing at him, said, "This man also was with him." But he denied it, saying, "Woman, I do not know him." And a little later some one else saw him and said, "You also are one of them." But Peter said, "Man, I am not." And after an interval of about an hour still another insisted, saying, "Certainly this man also was with him; for he is a Galilean." But Peter said, "Man, I do not know what you are saying." And immediately, while he was still speaking, the cock crowed. And the Lord turned and looked at Peter. And Peter remembered the word of the Lord, how he had said to him, "Before the cock crows today, you will deny me three times." And he went out, and wept bitterly.

[Slide of Christ before Pilate]

Reader #2 (Mark 15:6-15)
Now at the feast [the governor] used to release for them any one prisoner whom they asked. And among the rebels in prison, who had committed murder in the insurrection, there was a man called Barabbas. And the crowd came up and began to ask Pilate to do as he was wont to do for them. And he answered them, "Do you want me to release for you the King of the Jews?" For he perceived that it was out of envy that the chief priests had delivered him up. But the chief priests stirred up the crowd to have him release for them Barabbas instead. And Pilate again said to them, "Then what shall I do with the man whom you call the King of the Jews?" And they cried out again, "Crucify him." And Pilate said to them, "Why, what evil has he done?" But they shouted all the more, " Crucify him." So Pilate, wishing to satisfy the crowd, released for them Barabbas; and having scourged Jesus, he delivered him to be crucified.

ANTHEM [or congregational singing]
"Cross of Jesus, Cross of Sorrow"
[or other suitable music]

[Slide of Christ on cross]

READING OF SCRIPTURE
Reader #1 (Mark 15:22-24)
And they brought him to the place called Golgotha (which means the place of a

	skull). And they offered him wine mingled with myrrh; but he did not take it. And they crucified him.
Reader #2	(Luke 23:44-45a) It was now about the sixth hour, and there was darkness over the whole land until the ninth hour, while the sun's light failed. (Matthew 27:51b-54) And the earth shook, and the rocks were split; the tombs also were opened, and many bodies of the saints who had fallen asleep were raised, and coming out of the tombs after his resurrection they went into the holy city and appeared to many. When the centurion and those who were with him, keeping watch over Jesus, saw the earthquake and what took place, they were filled with awe, and said, "Truly this was a son of God!"
Reader #1	(Luke 23:45b) And the curtain of the temple was torn in two.
Reader #2	(Matthew 27:35b-36) They divided his garments among them by casting lots; then they sat down and kept watch over him there.
Reader #1	(Luke 23:50-56) Now there was a man named Joseph from the Jewish town of Arimathea. He was a member of the council, a good and righteous man, who had not consented to their purpose and deed, and he was looking for

the kingdom of God. This man went to Pilate and asked for the body of Jesus. Then he took it down . . .
[Slide of empty cross]
and laid him in a rock-hewn tomb, where no one had ever yet been laid. It was the day of Preparation, and the sabbath was beginning. The women who had come with him from Galilee followed, and saw the tomb, and how his body was laid; then they returned, and prepared spices and ointments.
On the sabbath they rested according to the commandment.

*HYMN   *"In the Cross of Christ I Glory"*

*BENEDICTION
Now may the Christ who shared his cup in communion and the Christ who suffered and died for us, dwell within us that we too might share the sorrow of sin. Amen

POSTLUDE

Maundy Thursday Meditation
Life's Upper Rooms

Matthew 26:17-30

Introduction:

Jesus has sent the disciples to prepare for the observance of the Passover. They are to meet a man carrying a jar of water to direct them to an upper room. They obey him; the room is found and all is prepared.

1. The Upper Room of Humility and Cleansing

One of the things the disciples had not even thought of was a common courtesy of a household. After weary travelers had traveled the dusty roads, they would take off their sandals and a servant of the household, or the host, would take a basin of water and a towel and wash the feet of the guests. Only Jesus would think of it. He took a towel and began to soothe the tired feet of his disciples with cool, refreshing water, and dry them. Some of them did not approve of him being their servant. Peter, of course, objected the loudest. When he found out the Lord meant business, he wanted the Lord to wash all of him. When masters become servants, they humble themselves to the most menial task in order that cleansing might come. We are charged to so act.

2. The Upper Room of Quiet Strength

It was a place of prayer. In the fellowship about the table, they prayed the prayers of their fathers and shared a common faith. They remembered what God had done for Israel and for them. The still, small voice of God would speak to them of greatness. It was a time and place where the tumult of the world, for a moment, would die away into silence, the ambitions of the world would shrink, and men would talk with their God.

And they would meet the Christ face to face. We all need to draw apart to be in silence with our God.

3. The Upper Room of Sacrifice

As they rehearsed again the drama of the Exodus, the deliverance of God's people from slavery, they remembered the sacrifice of innocent lambs. The angel of death had passed over their homes. They were free from Pharaoh's grasp. The kinds of food that were a part of their meal were symbols of sacrifice. Unleavened bread, bitter herbs, haroses, the lamb, were all evidence of God's willingness to deliver them. And now the disciples with Jesus celebrated what would be his last supper with them before he dies.

The ancient rite takes an unexpected turn. Jesus identifies the lamb, the unleavened bread, the fruit of the vine as his own. He tells them again of his impending sacrifice. Like the suffering servant of Isaiah 53 he, too, shall be led away as a lamb to the slaughter. It is anathema for them to think of it happening to Jesus.

Like the disciples, we also are to take and eat and drink, knowing full well that Jesus, embodied in us, leads us to sacrifice ourselves for his Kingdom.

4. The Upper Room of Refuge

After the crucifixion, the disciples are found in an upper room with the doors shut. It may be presumed to be locked, for the disciples are there out of fear and trembling for their own lives. It is into the room of refuge that the risen Christ comes, and comforts those who fear to go out and be the witnesses he needs. We, too, hide when we fear. Into that room of fear, Jesus will come.

5. The Upper Room of Contagious Hope

One day after the resurrection Jesus would gather with his disciples with a challenge to go into all the world and make disciples. It would no longer be a room of fear, but a room of contagious hope. From there they would go into all parts of the world, risking the dangers of hostile resistance to their message, but never losing hope. We follow that commandment yet today.

Good Friday

The worst possible happened to Jesus on the day we call Good Friday. He was tried before the Sanhedrin, then by Pilate, by Herod, and was then returned to Pilate; was scourged, mocked, and condemned to death. He then was taken by his oppressors to Golgotha, a skull-shaped hill outside the city wall, and crucified as a common criminal.

The value of this day lies in the promise of God to turn evil into good. God meant it for our salvation. "For God so loved the world that he gave his only Son, that whoever believes in him should not perish but have eternal life." (John 3:16) What was a day of sorrow and pain became, for all human beings, the open door to forgiveness, love, and new life. Through his sacrifice on the cross, we have salvation. That's what makes this Friday Good.

Good Friday

The Wounds of Christ

(*Congregation stand)

PRELUDE

*CALL TO WORSHIP

Leader: Surely he has borne our griefs and carried our sorrows;

Response: Upon him was the chastisement that made us whole, and with his stripes we are healed. (Isaiah 53:4,5)

Leader: And as Jesus was going up to Jerusalem, he took the twelve disciples aside, and on the way he said to them, "Behold, we are going up to Jerusalem; and the Son of man will be delivered to the chief priests and scribes, and they will condemn him to death, and deliver him to the Gentiles to be mocked and scourged and crucified, and he will be raised on the third day."
(Matthew 20:17-19)

The Wound of Betrayal

Pastor: Then one of the twelve, who was called Judas Iscariot, went to the chief priests and said, "What will you give me if I deliver him to you?" And they paid him thirty pieces of silver. And from that moment he sought an opportunity to betray him.

(Matthew 26:14-16)

All: *O Lord, like Judas, anxious that your Kingdom might come on earth as it is in heaven, we try to force your hand, thereby betraying you and your Kingdom.*

The Wound of Denial

Pastor: Simon Peter followed Jesus, and so did another disciple. As this disciple was known to the high priest, he entered the court of the high priest along with Jesus, while Peter stood outside at the door. So the other disciple, who was known to the high priest, went out and spoke to the maid who kept the door, and brought Peter in. The maid who kept the door said to Peter, "Are not you also one of this man's disciples?" He said, "I am not." Now the servants and officers had made a charcoal fire, because it was cold, and they were standing and warming themselves; Peter also was with them, standing and warming himself. Now Simon Peter was standing and warming himself. They said to him, "Are not you also one of his disciples?" He denied it and said, "I am not." One of the servants of the high priest, a kinsman of the man whose ear Peter had cut off, asked, "Did I not see you in the garden with him?" Peter again again denied it, and at once the cock crowed. (John 18:15-18, 25-27)

All: *Lord, like Peter, we offer our lives to you. But, when the test of our faith comes, we deny, by word and deed, that we know you.*

*HYMN "Beneath the Cross of Jesus"

The Wound of Misunderstanding

Pastor: Then Pilate took Jesus and scourged him. And the soldiers plaited a crown of thorns, and put it on his head, and arrayed him in a purple robe; they came up to him, saying, "Hail, King of the Jews!" and struck him with their hands.

(John 19:1-3)

Reader: **Pilate had asked Jesus if he were the King of the Jews. And Jesus answered, "My kingship is not of this world; if my kingship were of this world, my servants would fight, that I might not be handed over to the Jews; but my kingship is not from the world."** (John 18:36)
Not only did Pilate misunderstand Jesus' kingship, but also those closest to him, his disciples. People saw heavenly power in earthly terms: what Jesus could do for them. Some of them would have crowned him their earthly king, like David of old. They desired a conquering king that would recapture their earthly kingdom. Jesus wanted to be Lord of their hearts, to make God their Sovereign Ruler once more. A crown for Jesus would not be a golden one, but a thorny one, pressed upon the mind of one who knew clearly what kind of kingdom his Father ruled.

ALL: *O Lord, help us to follow you, not because of what you can do for us in earthly gain. Change our hearts that your Kingdom will help us grow into mature Christians.*

*HYMN [choir or congregation]
"O Sacred Head, Now Wounded"

The Wounded of Mockery

Pastor: And those who passed by derided him, wagging their heads and saying, "You who would destroy the temple and build it in three days, save yourself! If you are the Son of God, come down from the cross." So also the chief priests, with the scribes and elders, mocked him, saying, "He saved others; he cannot save himself. He is the King of Israel; let him come down now from the cross, and we will believe in him. He trusts in God; let God deliver him now, if he desires him; for he said, 'I am the Son of God.' "
(Matthew 27:39-43)

RESPONSIVE READING (Psalm 22:1-11)

Pastor: My God, my God, why hast thou forsaken me? Why art thou so far from helping me, from the words of my groaning? O my God, I cry by day, but thou dost not answer; and by night, but find no rest.

People: **Yet thou art holy, enthroned on the praises of Israel. In thee our fathers trusted; they trusted, and thou didst deliver them. To thee they cried, and were saved; in thee they trusted, and were not disappointed.**

Pastor: But I am a worm, and no man; scorned by men, and despised by the people. All who see me mock at me, they make mouths at me, they wag their heads; "He committed his cause to the Lord; let him deliver him, let him rescue him, for he delights in him!"

People: Yet thou art he who took me from the womb; thou didst keep me safe upon my mother's breasts. Upon thee was I cast from my birth, and since my mother bore me thou hast been my God.

All: *Be not far from me, for trouble is near and there is none to help.*

The Wounds of Hand and Feet

Pastor: So the soldiers came and broke the legs of the first, and of the other who had been crucified with him; but when they came to Jesus and saw that he was already dead, they did not break his legs. But one of the soldiers pierced his side with a spear, and at once there came out blood and water.

(John 19:32-34)

Reader: Now Thomas, one of the twelve, called the Twin, was not with them when Jesus came. So the other disciples told him, "We have seen the Lord." But he said to them, "Unless I see in his hands the print of the nails, and place my hand in his side, I will not believe."

Eight days later, his disciples were again in the house, and Thomas, was with them. The doors were shut, but Jesus came and stood among them, and said, "Peace be with you." Then he said to Thomas, "Put your finger here, and see my hands; and put out your hand, and place it in my side; do not be faithless, but believing." Thomas answered him, "My Lord and my God!" Jesus said to him, "Have you believed because you have seen me? Blessed are those who have not seen and yet believe."

(John 20:24-29)

MEDITATION *What Mean These Wounds to Me?*
*CALL TO DISCIPLESHIP

*CLOSING PRAYER

*BENEDICTION Behold, he is coming with the clouds, and every eye will see him, every one who pierced him; and all tribes of the earth will wail on account of him. Even so. Amen

(Revelation 1:7)

POSTLUDE

Community Service for Good Friday

PRELUDE

CHORAL INTROIT   "Let All Mortal Flesh Keep Silence"

*PROCESSIONAL   "The Church's One Foundation"

*INVOCATION

OLD TESTAMENT   Psalm 22:1-11, 25-31

PREFACE TO LITURGY   (Welcome and announcements)

Choosing

SCRIPTURE   John 15:16
You did not choose me, but I chose you and appointed you that you should go and bear fruit and that your fruit should abide.

*HYMN   "Jesus Calls Us"

LITANY

   Leader: (Deuteronomy 7:6)
For you are a people holy to the Lord your God; the Lord your God has chosen you to be a people for his own possession, out of all the peoples that are on the face of the earth.

   Response: We are yours, O Lord, we have heard your voice.

   Leader: (Exodus 19:5-6a)
Now therefore, if you will obey my voice and keep my covenant, you shall be my own possession among all peoples; for all the earth is mine, and you shall be to me a kingdom of priests and a holy nation.

Response: We are yours, O Lord, we have heard your voice.
Leader: (Leviticus 11:45)
For I am the Lord who brought you up out of the land of Egypt, to be your God; you shall therefore be holy, for I am holy.
Response: We are yours, O Lord, we have heard your voice.
Leader: (Colossians 3:12)
Put on then, as God's chosen ones, holy and beloved, compassion, kindness, lowliness, meekness, and patience.

Response: We accept your divine call — your will be done.
Leader: (1 Peter 2:4)
Come to him, to that living stone, rejected by men but in God's sight chosen and precious; and like living stones be yourselves built into a spiritual house, to be a holy priesthood, to offer spiritual sacrifices acceptable to God through Jesus Christ.
Response: We come, O Lord, to offer ourselves to you. Amen

OLD TESTAMENT (in unison)
Surely he has borne our griefs and carried our sorrows; yet we esteemed him stricken, smitten by God, and afflicted. But he was wounded for our transgressions, he was bruised for our iniquities; upon him was the chastisement that made us whole, and with his stripes we are healed. (Isaiah 53:4-5)

EPISTLE   1 Corinthians 26:31

COLLECT   (in unison)
Almighty God, we beseech you graciously to behold this your family, for which our Lord Jesus Christ was

content to be betrayed, given into the hands of wicked men, and to suffer death on the Cross; who now lives and reigns with you and the Holy Spirit, one God, world without end. Amen

DIALOGUE ON CHOOSING   *(God speaks to man)*

CHOIR ANTHEM   *"Go to Dark Gethsemane"*

Dying

SCRIPTURE   John 17:1-8

*HYMN   *"On a Hill Far Away"*

LITANY ON SEVEN LAST WORDS

Leader: (Luke 23:34a)
Father, forgive them; for they know not what they do.

Response: O Lord, absolve your people. Deliver us from our sins. Forgive our frailty, in Jesus' name.

Leader: (Luke 23:43b)
Today you will be with me in Paradise.

Response: O God, you are love; remember me.

Leader: (John 19:26b-27a)
Woman, behold your son . . . Behold your mother!

Response: May the bonds of love and ties of friendship be made stronger by him who, in mortal agony, was mindful of another's need.

Leader: (Matthew 27:46b)
My God, my God, why hast thou forsaken me?

Response: Help us, O Lord, to be so aware of your Word that in every circumstance of life we can turn to you.

Leader:	(John 19:28b) I thirst.
Response:	O Lord, increase our faith. Renew our courage. May our thirst be assuaged by the cup of blessing given by your Son.
Leader:	(John 19:30b) It is finished.
Response:	Almighty God, we beseech you that we, with all those who are departed in true faith, may have our perfect consummation and bliss in your eternal and everlasting glory, through Jesus Christ our Lord.
Leader:	(Luke 23:46) Father, into thy hands I commit my spirit!
Response:	O Lord, we offer and present to you ourselves, our souls and bodies, to be a reasonable, holy, and living sacrifice.

PRAYER OF CONFESSION (in unison)

We confess we are not our own, but yours, bought with a price. Therefore, O Lord, claim us as your right; keep us as your charge; and use us as you will, to the glory of your holy name and the good of of fellowman. Amen

SCRIPTURE   John 12:27, 32, 33

*HYMN   *"There Is a Green Hill Far Away"*

DIALOGUE (OR MESSAGE)*[Theme: Outside a City Wall]*

RESPONSIVE READING   [Based on hymn "Are Ye Able?"]
   Leader: "Are ye able?"
   (After leader reads each verse, let the people reply . . .)

Response:	Lord, we are able, our spirits are thine. Remold and make us like thee divine.
CHOIR ANTHEM	*"O Sacred Head, Now Wounded"*

Living

SCRIPTURE	John 3:16
HYMN	*"Lord, Speak to Me"* (verses 1, 2, 6)

LITANY

Leader:	(Galatians 6:14a) Far be it from me to glory except in the cross of our Lord Jesus.
Response:	In the cross of Christ I glory, Towering o'er the wrecks of time.
Leader:	(1 Peter 2:24a) He himself bore our sins in his body on the tree.
Response:	O love divine, what have you done! The incarnate God has died for me!
Leader:	(1 Peter 1:18a) You know that you were ransomed from the futile ways inherited from your fathers.
Response:	O sacred head, now wounded, with grief and shame weighed down.
Leader:	(1 Peter 3:18a) Christ died for sins once (and) for all, the righteous for the unrighteous, that he might bring us to God.
Response:	See from his head, his hands, his feet: sorrow and love flow mingled down. Did e'er such love and sorrow meet or thorns compose so rich a crown?

PRAYER (in unison)
By the remembrance of the suffering of our Lord Jesus Christ, we present ourselves, prepared in all humility, to be subject to the work of the Holy Spirit; that in living we be purged of pride and vainglory; in confession we may glorify God. Amen

SCRIPTURE John 15:12-17

*****HYMN** "Beneath the Cross of Jesus"

COLLECT FOR TODAY (in unison)
Let us run with perseverance the race that is set before us, looking to Jesus the pioneer and perfecter of our faith, who for the joy that was set before him endured the cross, despising the shame, and is seated at the right hand of the throne of God. (Hebrews 12:1b-2)

DIALOGUE (OR MESSAGE) *[Theme: It's Good Friday, the day Christ was crucified]*

*****HYMN** "I Know that My Redeemer Lives"

*****BENEDICTION**

POSTLUDE

A Good Friday Meditation

What About Saturday?

Luke 23:50-56

Introduction:
    It's Saturday
    And they've taken my Lord
    Down from the cross
    To a borrowed tomb.
    He lies there
    Wrapped in new linen and spices
    And I wait,
    Hoping God will touch and heal my sorrow.

There have been volumes written about Good Friday and Easter Sunday. Most of what's been written about Saturday could fill a thimble.

What really happened on the day that is sometimes called Holy or Light Saturday? We might guess that it was anything but a Holy Saturday for the disciples, for those who had learned to love him.

The Scriptures tell us that Jesus died on a Friday afternoon, just before the Jewish Sabbath day was to begin. It was called the Day of Preparation. If Jesus' body were not removed from the cross soon it would have to wait until after the Sabbath. That would have been anathema to the Jews. Joseph of Arimathea, a disciple who had been part of the Sanhedrin, silent until now, goes to claim Jesus' body from Pilate and offers his nearby tomb for his burial. When Pilate finds that Jesus is already dead, he gives the body to Joseph and to Nicodemus. They wrap Jesus' body in linen and myrrh and place him in the garden tomb. The women that followed Jesus are not allowed to be a part of the ceremony, because it is law that they cannot be near members of the Sanhedrin. They wait and watch.

"On the sabbath they rested according to the commandment." (Luke 23:56b)

1. On the Sabbath They Rested According to the Commandment

They were a people of the Law. They would obey the ordinance. However, we cannot help but wonder what was going on inside them.

Alfred Edersheim, in his great book, *The Life and Times of Jesus the Messiah*, writes: "on the holy Sabbath, when the officials were thinking of how to make sure of the dead Christ, what were the thoughts of Joseph of Arimathea and Nicodemus, of Peter and John, of the other disciples, and especially of the loving women who only waited for the first streak of Easter light to do their last service of love? What were their thoughts of God — what of the words He had spoken, the deeds He had wrought, the salvation He had come to bring." (p. 620, Book V, Vol. 2)

Matthew 27:62-66 tells us that on the sabbath the tomb was sealed and guarded. The soldiers would make sure no one would steal Jesus' body and claim a resurrection. But upon those who loved him, the shadows of death, sorrow, and grief had fallen. And great was the weight of it all.

2. Saturday, the Shadows Fell

Saturday for the disciples was one where Christ was absent. Fear, loneliness, despair, and doubt colored their thoughts and their actions. It was for them "the dark night of the soul," when you feel forsaken of God and every one else. Perhaps Joseph and Nicodemus felt guilt that they had been silent for so long. They may have felt remorse that they had not been more bold in their love and witness for him; perhaps they could have prevented his death. Peter, guilty of denying him, disillusioned by it all, decided to forget by returning to what he knew best, fishing. He and the other disciples would return to Galilee, back home where they ventured from only three short years ago.

Those disciples who looked on from afar were scared. They huddled together in a locked room, fearing for their very lives. John was trying to comfort Mary, the mother of Jesus. He had taken her to his own home as Jesus had bade him. The women who loved him waited out that Sabbath painfully, planning to go in the early morning hours to pay their respects, to further prepare his body for death.

It was not a good day.

3. Descent into Hell

> The earliest known form of the Apostles' Creed reads: *I believe in God the Father Almighty; and in Christ Jesus, His only begotten Son, our Lord, who was born of the Holy Spirit and the Virgin Mary, crucified under Pontius Pilate and buried; the third day He rose from the dead, ascended into the heavens, being seated at the right hand of the Father, whence He shall come to judge the living and the dead; and in the Holy Spirit, holy church, forgiveness of sins, resurrection of the flesh.* (from Williston Walker's *A History of the Christian Church*, p. 61)

In the most recent version of the creed, traditional use includes the words: "He descended into hell," after "was crucified, dead, and buried." There is some tradition that he descended into hell, the grave, to minister to those dead who had not known Christ and to bring them to salvation. In most Protestant churches this is not a part of their creed or theology. The traditional belief that he descended into hell took place between his death and his resurrection. An ancient homily used on Holy Saturday indicates that Jesus went searching in hell for our first parents, Adam and Eve. It states that the Lord approached Adam, carrying his cross, the weapon of his victory over death and sin. At the sight of Christ, Adam is to have said, "My Lord be with you all." And Christ responded: "And with your spirit." He then took Adam by the hand to raise him up, and said, "Awake, O sleeper, and rise from the dead, and Christ will give you light."

4. What About Our Saturdays?

There are the times when fear, despair, depression, loneliness, doubt, grip us and hold us in their sway. There seems to be no comfort or strength.

Illness strikes and we fear for our life. We stand at the grave of a loved one and feel the shadows. A girl who is otherwise beautiful has scars on her face from disease, and wonders if anyone will ever love her. A man loses a job and knows he is too old by company standards to train for something else. We stand by the bed of loved ones and see them dying and are utterly helpless to do anything about it. The illustrations go on and on. It's Saturday.

5. What Makes Saturdays Really Saturdays Is That We Forget What We Have Believed About God's Presence in Our Lives

If the disciples really believed Jesus would rise from the dead, they would not have panicked. Their fears and everything else would not have been so heavy.

6. It Is Christ Who Comes to Deliver Us From Our Saturdays

We are able to see through the bad times when we build reservoirs of trust with God beforehand. It was Jesus who entered locked doors. Even when the disciples, the women, other followers are in sorrow, God is there to see them through Saturday. He can do that for us, too. Saturday becomes holy for us when we realize that God has not left us alone.

www.ingramcontent.com/pod-product-compliance
Lightning Source LLC
Chambersburg PA
CBHW060858050426
42453CB00008B/1008